THE MEL SIMONS JOKE BOOK

To Bill —
May you live to be as old as some of these jokes!
Mel Simons

Also by Mel Simons:

The Old-Time Radio Trivia Book

The Old-Time Television Trivia Book

Old-Time Radio Memories

The Show-Biz Trivia Book

Old-Time Television Memories

The Movie Trivia Book

Voices from the Philco

The Good Music Trivia Book

THE MEL SIMONS JOKE BOOK
IF IT'S LAUGHTER YOU'RE AFTER

BY MEL SIMONS

BearManor Media
2013

The Mel Simons Joke Book:
If It's Laughter You're After

© 2013 Mel Simons

All rights reserved.

For information, address:

BearManor Media
P. O. Box 71426
Albany, GA 31708

bearmanormedia.com

Typesetting and layout by John Teehan

Published in the USA by BearManor Media

ISBN — 1-59393-243-X
978-1-59393-243-5

Dedication

*This book is dedicated to Bob Elliott.
I have loved the comedy team of Bob & Ray my entire life.
Bob has become a very special friend.*

Mel Simons

The Mel Simons Joke Book

Steven Wright and Mel Simons

Foreword

This book is full of excellent jokes and is just so enjoyable and fun to read. It's like going on a little ride away from your real life. I laughed out loud many times. Some comedians you may know of, but are not really familiar with their specific material. This is a fun way to experience these legends. There are also fantastic street jokes that are hilarious. Mel Simons has put together a great collection of pure funny material from many, many excellent comedians. Very enjoyable, and something you'll love to read over again, and share with other people. I highly recommend it.

– Steven Wright

Preface

"If It's Laughter You're After," you've come to the right place.

We've all heard that "laughter is the best medicine" and I put together this book of jokes to help keep my readers happy and laughing.

This book of jokes includes:

SOMETHING OLD

SOMETHING NEW

SOMETHING BORROWED

NOTHING BLUE

You will be reading a "clean" joke book that will keep you smiling and even laughing out loud. The book is an "equal opportunity" offender, complete with "Irish," "Italian," and "Jewish" jokes, and "Doctor," "Lawyer," and "Drunk" jokes.

The book also pays tribute to the great comedians of the 20th century, including Milton Berle, Morey Amsterdam, Henny Youngman and Rodney Dangerfield. I have had the honor of introducing all of these gentlemen during my years as MC at

The Mel Simons Joke Book

the famed Hotel Brickman in New York's Catskill Mountains. The book includes photos of some of these great men of comedy, many of them autographed to me.

I have had a love affair with the great comedians since I was a kid. I have followed them throughout their careers. They may have left us, but their comedy remains alive for us to enjoy to this day.

Jokes

A woman goes to a fortune teller. The fortune teller said, "Your husband will die a violent death." The woman said, "When will I be acquitted?"

A husband and wife are in bed at night. He starts to rub her shoulder. He starts to rub her stomach. He starts to rub her hip. Suddenly, he stops. She said, "Why did you stop?" He said, "I found the remote."

Two people were found frozen to death in their car at a drive-in movie theater. They had gone to see "CLOSED FOR THE WINTER."

Two old friends meet on the street. One says to the other, "I think my wife died." His friend said, "What do you mean you *think* she died?" "Well, the sex is the same, but the dishes are piling up in the sink."

The Mel Simons Joke Book

Mel Simons and Henny Youngman

Henny Youngman Jokes

Two guys were in a gym. One started to put on a girdle. One guy says, "Since when have you been wearing a girdle?" The other guy says, "Since my wife found it in the glove compartment of our car."

My doctor told me I was fat. I said I wanted a second opinion. He said, "OK, you're ugly too."

If you're going to do something tonight that you'll be sorry for tomorrow, sleep late.

Last night I set up a mousetrap with a picture of cheese. I caught a picture of a mouse.

They usually have two clerks in my local Post Office, except when it's very busy. Then they have one.

I once wanted to be an atheist, but I gave it up because they have no holidays.

The Mel Simons Joke Book

My wife wanted to get a face lift. They couldn't do that, so they lowered her body.

I said to my mother-in-law, "My house is your house." Last week she sold it.

This morning my wife ran after the garbage truck. She yelled, "Am I too late for the garbage?" The garbage man yelled back, "No, jump in."

A guy walked up to me and said, "Have you seen any cops around here?" I said, "No." He said, "Stick em up." I said, "Stick what up?" He said, "Don't mix me up. It's my first job."

My wife went to the beauty parlor and got a mud pack. For three days she looked great. Then the mud fell off.

My wife found a furrier who does his own breeding. He crossed a mink with a gorilla. The fur coat is beautiful, but the sleeves are too long.

I just came back from a pleasure trip. I took my mother-in-law to the airport.

Henny Youngman Jokes

A drunk was in front of a judge. The judge says, "You've been brought here for drinking." The drunk says, "OK, let's get started."

I bought my wife a new car. Three weeks ago she learned how to drive it. Last week she learned how to aim it.

My brother-in-law tells people that he's a diamond cutter. He mows the lawn at Yankee Stadium.

I'm not saying my wife is a terrible cook, but our garbage disposal has developed an ulcer.

Yesterday my wife backed the car out of the garage. What she didn't know was that I had backed it in.

My grandmother is over eighty and still doesn't need glasses. She drinks right out of the bottle.

My best friend ran away with my wife, and let me tell you, I miss him.

Doctor: "You'll live to be 60."
Patient: "I am 60."
Doctor: "See, what did I tell you?"

The Mel Simons Joke Book

I've been in love with the same woman for forty five years. If my wife finds out, she'll kill me.

Why does the Italian Navy have glass bottom boats?
So they can see the old Italian Navy.

Why don't Jews drink?
It interferes with their suffering.

A woman is taking a shower. Her doorbell rings. She yells, "Who's there?" He says, "Blind man." She happens to be a very charitable lady. She jumps out of the shower, stark naked, and opens the door. He says, "Where should I put these blinds, lady?"

I dreamt that God sneezed. I didn't know what to say to him.

Jewish Foreplay: Three hours of begging.
Italian Foreplay: "Maria, I'm home."

Jokes

A Catholic, Protestant, and Jewish patient are in the hospital. They are about to die. The doctor asked each one to make a last wish. The Catholic wanted to make a confession. The Protestant wanted to see his family for the last time. The Jew said, "I want to see another doctor."

Walter came home and found his wife in bed with his best friend. He walked over to his friend and said, "Sam, I have to, but you?"

A man went to visit his elderly father. The father was watching television.
Son: "Hi, Pop. What are you watching?"
Father: "Basketball."
Son: "What's the score?"
Father: "86 to 82."
Son: "Who's winning?"
Father: "86."

Questions & Answers

What has 200 legs and six teeth?
The front row of a Willie Nelson concert

What do you call a nun that walks in her sleep?
A Roman Catholic

What do you call a woman who always knows where her husband is?
A widow

Why did the Siamese twins move to London?
So the other one could drive

Why did Moses wander in the desert for 40 years?
He was using Map Quest

What's the difference between a drunk and an alcoholic?
A drunk doesn't have to go to the meetings.

Questions & Answers

What do you get when you cross a Jehovah's Witness with an Atheist?
Someone who rings your doorbell for no reason

What do you give an elephant with diarrhea?
Lot of room

What are the three ages of man?
Youth, middle age, and "My, don't you look good."

Why did the golfer wear two pairs of pants?
He got a hole in one

What do you get when you cross an elephant and a prostitute?
A hooker who does it for peanuts and will never forget you

Steven Wright Jokes

Steven never fails to make me laugh. He is one of my favorite comedians. Here are five of his gems:

I hate when my foot falls asleep during the day, because that means it's going to be up all night.

I put instant coffee into a microwave oven and almost went back in time.

Why are ballerinas always on their tip toes? Why don't they just get taller women?

Sponges grow in the ocean. I wonder how much deeper the ocean would be if that didn't happen?

I used to work in a factory that made hydrants. You couldn't park anywhere near the place!

Irish Jokes

What's an Irish seven course meal?
A six pack and a potato

Did you hear about the man that was half Irish and half Scottish? Half of him wants to get drunk, and the other half doesn't want to pay for it.

A little Irish boy said to a little Jewish boy, "My priest knows more than your rabbi." The little Jewish boy said, "He should, you tell him everything."

What's the difference between an Irish wedding and an Irish funeral?
One less drunk

Patrick and Kevin meet in a pub in Dublin. Kevin said, "Did you hear what happened to Sullivan? He's dead." Patrick said, "Oh my, what happened?" Kevin said, "He was working in a brewery. He fell into a big vat of ale, and he drowned." Patrick said, "Well at least he went quickly." Kevin said, "Well, not really. He climbed out three times to pee."

The Jews invented guilt, and the Irish turned it into an art form.

The Mel Simons Joke Book

An Irish immigrant decides to go to night school. He wants to improve his English. The teacher said to him, "Tell me, who said these words: 'TO BE OR NOT TO BE?'" He said, "Somebody calling Bingo."

Why did the Irishman have his toes amputated?
So he could stand closer to the bar

Recently in Ireland, workmen were demolishing an old house. In an upstairs closet they found a skeleton with a medal around its neck. The inscription on the medal read: "Dublin 1923 Hide and Seek Champion."

A guy from New York walks into a tavern in Ireland and says, "I'll give $500 to any man who can drink ten pints of Guinness in ten minutes." Riley runs out of the bar and comes back six minutes later. He says, "I'll take that challenge." He then drinks all ten pints in seven minutes. The New Yorker asked, "Where did you go when you left here?" Riley said, "Around the corner to another bar. I had to see if it could be done."

Mary Cassidy went to see her priest, Father Sullivan. She was shaking and crying. She said, "Father, something terrible has happened. My husband died." Father Sullivan said, "Oh, I'm so sorry, Mary. Did he have a last request?" She said, "Yes, Father. He said, 'For God's sake, Mary, put down that gun.'"

Irish Jokes

Did you hear about the Irishman that read so many bad things about drinking that he decided to give up reading?

Clancy has had a little too much to drink. He's sitting in his parked car, and he's yelling, "Look what they did to my car. I can't believe it. Look what they did to my car." A cop walks by and says, "What seems to be the problem?" Clancy said, "Officer, look what they did to my car. They stole my steering wheel, they stole my radio, they stole my glove compartment." The cop said, "You're sitting in the back seat."

What is 84 feet wide, a quarter of a mile long, and has an IQ of 30?
The St. Patrick's Day Parade

Three Irishmen were standing at a bar having a few brews. Suddenly the front door opened, and in walked Father O'Brien. The good Father walked over to the three men and said to the first one, "Do you want to go to heaven?" The first guy said, "Yes, I do." Father O'Brien said to the second man, "Do you want to go to heaven?" The guy said, "Yes, I do." Father O'Brien then said to the third man, "How about you? Do you want to go to heaven?" The guy said, "No." Father O'Brien said, "Do you mean to tell me that when you die, you don't want to go to heaven?" The guy said, "Oh, when I die, I thought you were picking up a load right now!"

The Mel Simons Joke Book

On a tombstone in Ireland, there is this inscription:

Here lies the body of John O'Rourke
Two bullets made him clay,
He lived the life of Riley,
While Riley was away

A young Irish priest had just gotten ordained. He was in his mid-twenties, and looked like he was fourteen years old. He was driving his car, going about eighty five miles per hour. A big Irish cop pulled him over and started to write out a ticket. The young priest looked out of the car window, with this young innocent face, and said, "But I'm Father Fox." The cop said, "I don't care if you're Mother Goose, you're getting a ticket."

Pat and Mike left Ireland to have a visit with the Pope in Italy. When they arrived in Italy, they stopped at a tavern to have a drink. The Italian bartender said, "What would you gentlemen like to drink?" Pat said, "Give us a couple of pints of Guinness Stout." The Italian bartender said, "We don't serve Guinness Stout over here." "Well," Pat asked, "what does the Pope drink?" The bartender said, "Benedictine and Brandy." Pat said, "Give Mike and I a pint each." Pat and Mike drank it down, and it was very strong. Pat looked at Mike and said, "No wonder they have to carry that guy around in a chair."

Name seven Irish days that are celebrated with a lot of drinking.
Monday, Tuesday, Wednesday, Thursday, Friday, Saturday, Sunday

Irish Jokes

An Irishman from the south of Ireland has just arrived in New York City. This is his first visit to the United States, and he's strolling down Fifth Avenue. This being his first trip here, he is not familiar with the traffic regulations. He starts to cross the street against the green light. A big Irish cop yells, "Hey, get back, my good man. Don't you know any better than to cross when the light is green? When it turns red, you can cross. Red is the color for you to cross on." The Irishman stands on the corner for a few moments. He watches the green light for a while. Then he sees it turn yellow for a few seconds, and then red. As he starts to cross the street, he says to the cop, "They don't give the Protestants much time, do they?"

What's Irish and stays out all night?
Paddy O'Furniture

Finnegan walked into a bar in Dublin. His nose was bloody, and he was black and blue all over. The bartender said, "My God, what happened to you? You look terrible." Finnegan said, "I had a fight with Kevin Gallagher." The bartender said, "You let a little guy like Kevin Gallagher beat you up. You should be ashamed of yourself, a little no good guy like Kevin." "Hold on there," said Finnegan, "don't be talking disrespectfully of the dead."

Father McDonald looked over the class and asked little Shean, "Do you say a prayer before meals in your house?" "We don't have to, Father. My mother is a good cook."

The Mel Simons Joke Book

Sunday morning, in church, Father Feeny was talking to his congregation about the suddenness of death. He said, "Before this day is over, somebody in this parish could die." Brian Hagerty, sitting in the first row, started to laugh out loud. "What's so funny?" asked Father Feeny. Brian yelled, "I'm not a member of this parish."

Dennis and Pat have been great friends for eighty eight years. They came to this country together, from Ireland, over sixty years ago. Now Pat is on his deathbed, and his old pal, Dennis, is by his side. Slowly, Pat opens his eyes and says, "Dennis, me boy, it's almost over for me. I wonder if you'd do me one last favor. When I'm gone, would you take that bottle of Irish whiskey in me closet, and pour it over me grave?" Dennis said, "Pat, I'd be only too happy to do that for you. But would you mind if I let it pass through me kidneys first?"

What is dining out for an Irishman?
Eating a TV dinner on the front porch

A very pompous Englishman hailed a cab in New York City. In a very arrogant manner, he said to the Irish cab driver, "Take me to Christ Church immediately." The cab driver took him across town, and stopped at St. Patrick's Cathedral. As the man was getting out of the cab, he looked up and said, "This isn't Christ Church." The cab driver said, "Look, Mac, if he ain't in there, he ain't in town!"

Drunk Jokes

Two drunks were walking along railroad tracks. One turned to the other and said, "This is the longest flight of stairs I ever climbed." The other one said, "It's not the steps I mind. It's these low banisters."

Two drunks go to the zoo. They're standing in front of the lion's cage. All of a sudden, the lion lets out a great big roar. One drunk turns to the other and says, "Let's get out of here." The other one says, "We can't leave now. The picture just started."

A drunk staggered up to a parking meter, inserted a quarter, and shouted, "My God, I lost a hundred pounds!"

"Pardon me," the drunk asked the hostess, "but does a lemon have feathers?" The hostess said, "Don't be ridiculous, of course not." The drunk said, "I think I just squeezed your canary into my drink."

Dean Martin used to say, "I only drink to steady my nerves. Last night I got so steady, I couldn't move."

The Mel Simons Joke Book

This guy was the town drunk. He drank so much that many times he couldn't see straight. He decided to go to confession. He opened the door to the booth, went inside, and sat down. He said, "Bless me father, for I have sinned. Sometimes I drink so much, I don't know where I am." The voice at the next booth said, "You're sitting on the toilet seat in the men's room!"

Bartenders have been making a new drink. It's made with vodka and carrot juice. You get drunk just as fast, but your eyesight gets better.

Two drunks were walking along Fifth Avenue in New York City. One goes down into the subway by mistake. He comes up five minutes later, and his friend is waiting for him. The friend says, "Where the heck were you?" He said, "I was in some guy's basement. Boy has he got a set of trains!"

A pompous lady is sitting at a bar. An obnoxious drunk sits down beside her, and continues to drink. The lady says, "If you were my husband, I would poison your drink." The drunk answered, "If you were my wife, I would drink it."

Two drunk guys went bear hunting. They got on the highway and saw a sign: BEAR LEFT. So they went home.

Drunk Jokes

A drunk walks into an empty elevator shaft. He falls down nine flights. He picks himself up, dusts himself off, and says, "I guess I should have said up."

A man walks into a bar and says to the bartender, "Give me ten shots of scotch, make it doubles." He then proceeds to drink them all in one minute. The bartender says, "My God, I have never seen anybody drink like that." The man said, "Well, you'd drink like this if you had what I have." The bartender said, "What do you have?" The man said, "Fifty cents."

A husband and wife were staying at a hotel. It's 2:00 in the morning. They are sleeping. Suddenly there's a knock on the door. The husband opened the door, and there's a drunk standing there. The drunk says, "Gee, I'm sorry." The husband slams the door, and jumps back into bed. Five minutes later, another knock on the door. The husband opens the door, it's that same drunk. The drunk says, "Gee, I'm really sorry." The husband slams the door, jumps back in bed again. Five minutes later, another knock on the door. He opens the door. The drunk says, "What did you do, rent every room on this floor?"

The Mel Simons Joke Book

Red Buttons

Red Buttons Jokes

Amelia Earhart, who once said, "Never mind looking for me, find my luggage"…never got a dinner.

King Solomon, who told his thousand wives, "For better service, take a number"…never got a dinner.

Venus de Milo's mother, who said to Venus, "What, you can't pick up a phone"…never got a dinner.

Eve, who said to Adam in the Garden of Eden, "What do you mean the kids don't look like you"…never got a dinner.

Francis Scott Key's wife, who said to Francis, "Why don't you write a song we can listen to sitting down"…never got a dinner.

Paul Revere, who wore nothing but a raincoat, and said, "I will flash once if by land, and twice if by sea"…never got a dinner.

The Mel Simons Joke Book

The invisible man's mother-in-law, who said to invisible, "I don't know what my daughter sees in you"…never got a dinner.

Abraham Lincoln's wife, who said, "Abe, why don't we wait and see it on TV"…never got a dinner.

Bluebeard, who said to Scotland Yard, "How do I know how many women I've killed. I'm a murderer, not an accountant"…never got a dinner.

Thomas Edison's mother, who said to Thomas, "I don't know what you're doing in there, but I can't sleep with the lights on"…never got a dinner.

Mrs. Paul Revere, who said to Paul, "You are not! I'm gonna use the horse tonight"…never got a dinner.

Napoleon's mother, who said, "I told you a thousand times, stop scratching and the rash will go away"…never got a dinner.

Moses, who said when the Red Sea parted, "I was only going in for a dip"…never got a dinner.

Red Buttons Jokes

Steven Spielberg's mother, who said to E.T. "I don't care where you're from. You're here now, and you're gonna be Bar Mitzvah'd"…never got a dinner.

Wilt Chamberlain's mother, who once said, "Kids don't look up to their parents anymore"…never got a dinner.

Methuselah, who lived to be 900 years old, and he didn't get one card from his kids…never got a dinner.

Orson Welles, who once told Ethel Merman to speak up… never got a dinner.

Jack the Ripper's mother, who said to Jack, "How come I never see you with the same girl twice"…never got a dinner.

The Mel Simons Joke Book

Jokes

A man decides to go ice fishing. He chops a hole in the ice, drops his line, and starts to fish. Suddenly he hears a voice, "There are no fish in the water." He looks around, and there's nobody around. He continues to fish, and again he hears the voice, "There are no fish in the water." He thinks it is God talking to him. He says, "Is that you, God?" And the voice says, "This is the manager of the ice skating rink."

Two elderly men were watching a funeral procession go by.
1st man: "Who died?"
2nd man: "I think it was the gentleman in the first car."

A lady was browsing in an art museum. She came to a large gold frame that was mounted on the wall. She said to the curator, "This is the worst thing I have ever seen. Is this what they call modern art?" He said, "No, this is a mirror."

Loser Jokes

A loser is…

A man who saves up all his life for a cemetery plot and then drowns at sea.

An accordion player in a topless girl band.

A guy who was the lookout at Pearl Harbor.

A woman who loves to have sex in the back seat of their car, and she wants her husband to drive.

A man who gets a kidney transplant from a chronic bed wetter.

A girl who puts on her bra backwards, and it fits.

A guy who sticks his hand out to make a left turn, and hits a cop right in the mouth.

A newlywed who carries his bride over the threshold and gets a hernia.

A man who opens his fortune cookie and finds a draft notice.

The Mel Simons Joke Book

A peeping tom who looks through a keyhole and sees another eye.

A guy who puts a seashell to his ear and gets a busy signal.

A Hindu snake charmer with a deaf cobra.

A man who dies and they cremate him. On the way to the cemetery, the hearse gets stuck in the snow and they have to use his ashes to get the hearse out of the snow.

A piano player in a marching band.

A lady who tries to give a drowning man mouth to mouth, and he refuses.

Milton Berle Jokes

The Italians and the Jews have a lot in common. It was an Italian who invented the toilet seat, but it was a Jew who had brains enough to put a hole in it.

I joined an organization that fights inflation. An hour after I joined, they raised the dues.

I said to my wife, "Do you feel that the excitement has gone out of our marriage?" She said, "I'll discuss it with you during the next commercial break."

Milton Berle and Mel Simons

The Mel Simons Joke Book

We owe a lot to Thomas Edison. If it wasn't for him, we'd be watching television by candlelight.

A man falls down a flight of stairs. Somebody rushes over to him and asks, "Did you miss a step?" "No," he answers, "I hit every one of them!"

I told my wife that black underwear turns me on. So she didn't wash my shorts for three months.

I asked my doctor what to do for a sprained ankle. He said, "Limp."

Waiting for Dean Martin to stop drinking is like leaving the porch light on for Jimmy Hoffa.

I just closed a very successful engagement in Mexico. I performed for the Kaopectate Convention. It was a very long run!

A friend of mine belongs to Alcoholics Anonymous. He's not a fanatic about it. He doesn't go to meetings. He just sends in his empties.

Where I live, we don't worry about crime in the streets. They make house calls.

Milton Berle Jokes

Clint Eastwood is the only guy who comes back from Mexico constipated.

A young man fills out an application for a job. He does well until he gets to the last question, "Who should we notify in case of an accident?" He mulls it over and then writes, "Anybody in sight."

Your marriage is in trouble if your wife says, "You're only interested in one thing," and you can't remember what it is.

I can't tell you how old my brother is, but when he was born, the wonder drug was Mercurochrome.

I know a guy who is so old, that when he orders a three minute egg, they make him pay up front.

Mel Simons and Milton Berle

Jokes

A man rushed to his psychiatrist yelling, "I'm a teepee. I'm a wigwam. I'm a teepee. I'm a wigwam!" "Calm down," said the psychiatrist, "you're two tents."

A guy is staying in a hotel. He calls the front desk and says to the clerk, "I've gotta leak in my sink." The clerk said, "Go ahead."

Gas prices are so high, that during a high speed chase on the New York Freeway, the cops and the crooks were in the same car.

A married couple is sleeping. In the middle of the night, the phone rings. She says, "Answer it." He gets on the phone, he says, "Hello, why don't you call the Coast Guard?" He hangs up. She said, "Who was it?" He said, "Some fella wants to know if the coast is clear."

Limericks

There was an old woman from Kent
Whose nose was remarkably bent
One day they suppose
She followed her nose
And nobody knows where she went

There was a young girl from St. Paul
Wore a newspaper dress to a ball
But the dress caught on fire
And burned her entire
Front page, sporting section, and all

A dieting gal name Flynn
Reduced until she was thin
She's no more, I'm afraid
For she sipped lemonade
And slipped through the straw and fell in

There once was a man named O'Leary
When he drank, he became very cheery
As he left Murphy's Bar
He totaled his car
Now O'Leary ain't cheery, he's dreary

There was a young lady of Kent
Who said that she knew what it meant
When men took her to dine
Gave her cocktails and wine
She knew what it meant, but she went

There once was a man from St. Paul
Who went to a fancy dress ball
He said, "Yes, I'll risk it,
I'll go as a biscuit,"
And a dog ate him up in the hall

Jokes

A guy goes into a drugstore. The lady pharmacist says, "May I help you?" The guy says, "I'm a little embarrassed. Is there a male pharmacist I can speak to?" The lady says, "Please don't be embarrassed. My sister and I have owned this drugstore for 25 years. You can tell us anything." He said, "My problem is that I suffer from constant sexual arousal. What would you suggest?" She said, "Let me talk to my sister. I'll be right back." She comes back and says, "The best we can do is a thousand dollars a week and half of the store."

Bill and Bob go hunting in the woods. Bill suddenly falls down and it looks like he is not breathing. Bob calls 911 on his cell phone. He says to the operator, "I think my friend is dead. What should I do?" The operator said, "I can help you. Are you sure he's dead?" There's 15 seconds silence, and then a gunshot is heard. Bob comes back to the phone and says, "OK, now what?"

Daffynitions

OPERA – where a man gets stabbed in the back, and instead of bleeding, he sings

TIMEKEEPER – a person who didn't return your watch

METEOROLOGIST – a man who can look into a girl's eyes and tell weather

DENIAL – a river in Egypt

SCHLEMIEL – a guy who buys a suit with two pairs of pants, then burns a hole in the jacket

TERMINAL ILLNESS – when you are sick at the airport

CRITIC – a man who knows the way, but can't drive a car

DRY-DOCK – a physician who doesn't drink

BAGEL – a doughnut dipped in cement

Daffynitions

INFORMATION – how birds fly

RAVING BEAUTY – a lady who comes in last in a beauty contest

CHUTZPAH – a guy with a ski mask. He walks into a bank and holds up the teller. He then walks over to the next teller and says, "I want to open up an account."

RHUBARB – celery that is bloodshot

BARIUM – what you do when someone dies

NUDNIK – a naked Santa Claus

SHINBONE – a device for finding furniture in a dark room

The Mel Simons Joke Book

Morey Amsterdam

Morey Amsterdam Jokes

Two senior citizens are walking along Collins Avenue in Miami. They are walking in opposite directions. All of a sudden, they stop. One looks at the other. He says, "Sam, my God, you're still alive. I thought we were both dead."

My wife told me to buy big eggs in the supermarket. I brought them home. We broke them open. You know what was inside? Panty hose!

One day I saw my picture in the paper. Underneath the picture, it said that I had just died. I called the editor of the paper. I said, "This is Morey Amsterdam. I just saw my picture in the paper. It said I had died." He said, "I saw it too. Where are you calling from?"

I was on a subway the other day. A crazy man was running around, and he was yelling, "I'm George Washington, I'm George Washington." Everybody got panicky, but I saved the day. I yelled, "Next stop, Valley Forge," and he got off.

My wife is a terrible cook. How can you burn Jell-O? One night she made stuffed chicken. It was awful. I said to her, "What did you stuff it with?" She said, "Nothing, it wasn't empty."

A fellow goes to the doctor. Just as he gets there, the door flies open and a nun comes running out. As she's running down the hall, she is screaming, "No, no, no." I said, "Doctor, what's the matter? What happened with the nun?" He said, "I just told her she was pregnant." I said, "Is she?" He said, "No, but it sure cured her hiccups."

A fella went to see his doctor. He said, "Doctor, every time I look in the mirror, I throw up." The doctor said, "Hey, don't feel bad. Your eyes are good."

A fireman was pulling a drunk out of a burning bed.
Fireman: "You darn fool. That'll teach you to smoke in bed."
Drunk: "I wasn't smoking in bed. It was on fire when I laid down."

A man was in an elevator. The door opened and a girl walked in stark naked. She said, "What are you staring at?" He said, "Nothing. I just noticed my wife has the same outfit."

She said, "Kiss me, kiss me." He said, "Are you crazy? I'm a married man. I shouldn't even be doing this!"

It's easy to grin
When your ship comes in
And life is a happy lot
But the man worthwhile
Is the guy who can smile
When his shorts creep up in a knot

My brother's wife is so skinny
That when she puts on a strapless gown
She has to wear suspenders
To keep it from falling down

My mother and father keep fighting
They rant and they rave and they shout
"Who is your father?" somebody asked
"That's what they're fighting about."

The Mel Simons Joke Book

Mel Simons and Morey Amsterdam

Jokes

A man is driving his car on I-95. His cell phone rings. He picks it up. It's his wife. She says, "Sam, I just heard on the radio, there's one car on I-95 going the wrong way. Look out for that one car." He said, "One car, I see a hundred."

The other day I drove past a church in Boston. They had a big sign out front. "If you're tired of sin, come on in." Underneath it, someone wrote in lipstick, "If not, call 555-5217."

A lady went to the cemetery to visit her husband's tombstone. She looked all over the cemetery and couldn't find it. She went to the manager and said, "I can't find my husband's tombstone." He said, "What's his name?" She said, "Abe Merman." He looked in the book and said, "I haven't got an Abe Merman, but I have a Millie Merman." She said, "That's him. Everything is in my name."

Doctor Jokes

An 85 year old man married a 21 year old girl. He went to see his doctor. The old man said, "Could you give me something to give me a little more pizzazz?" The doctor gave him these little pills. The doctor said, "Take one pill every evening." That night he took the whole bottle. The next morning his wife tried to wake him. She said, "George, it's time to wake up." He opened his eyes and said, "I'll get up, but I won't go to school."

A man goes to a doctor. He says, "Doctor, it's terrible what I have been going through. I touch my elbow, it hurts. I touch my hip, it hurts. I touch my knee, it hurts. What's wrong with me?" The doctor said, "You have a broken finger."

An old man went to see his doctor. The doctor asked, "What's the problem?" The old man said, "I can't pee." The doctor asked, "How old are you?" The old man said, "I'm ninety eight." The doctor said, "You peed enough."

Nurse: "Doctor, the man that you just gave a clean bill of health to dropped dead outside your office door."
Doctor: "Turn him around. Make believe he's coming in."

Doctor Jokes

A man says, "Doctor, I'm having trouble with my love life. What should I do?" Doctor says, "Take off twenty pounds. Run ten miles a day." The man calls the doctor two weeks later. He says, "Doc, I took off twenty pounds. I'm running ten miles a day." Doctor asks, "Well, how's your love life?" Man says, "I don't know. I'm a hundred and forty miles away!"

This woman calls her doctor. She says, "Doctor, I have a terrible problem. Every day my husband goes into the bathroom with a fishing pole. He sits down on the bathtub, and fishes in the toilet." The doctor said, "Have you seen a psychologist about this?" She said, "No, I'm too busy cleaning fish."

A man goes to a doctor. He says, "My wife has been thinking of getting breast implants. Tell me about it." Doctor says, "It's a very common procedure. I can do it right here in the office. There is no pain. It will cost you $25,000. Go home and discuss it with your wife. Call me back in a day or two." The man goes home. He calls the doctor the next day and says, "We decided to redo the kitchen."

An old man goes to the doctor. He says, "I'm 92 years old doc, and I'm marrying a girl who is 22." The doctor said, "Forget it, she'll kill you." He said, "No, we're in love. We're gonna get married." The doctor said, "Well, all I can do is give you a little advice. Take in a boarder." He said, "All right, I'll do it." A few months later, the doctor meets the old man. The doctor asks, "How are things going with the marriage?" He says, "Terrific, my wife is pregnant." Doctor says, "What about the boarder?" He says, "She's pregnant too?"

A little grandmother is walking down the street. She bumps into her doctor. The doctor says, "Hello, Esther. How do you feel?" She says, "My blood pressure is not good, my arthritis is bothering me, and my stomach hurts." Doctor says, "Why don't you come to the office to see me?" She says, "Maybe next week when I feel better."

Did you hear about the doctor that gave a man six months to live? The man couldn't pay his bill, so the doctor gave him another six months.

This doctor called his patient and said, "I have some bad news and some terrible news for you." The patient said, "What's the bad news?" Doctor said, "You have 48 hours to live." Patient said, "Well, wait a minute. What's the terrible news?" Doctor said, "I've been looking for you for 2 days."

The doctor entered the waiting room. He said, "I have some good news for you, Mrs. Benson." "Pardon me," she said, "but it's Miss." The doctor said, "I have some bad news for you, Miss Benson."

Patient: "Doctor, I have a very bad problem. It's my memory. I can't remember anything."
Doctor: "How long have you had this problem?"
Patient: "What problem?"

Walter goes to a doctor and says, "Every time my wife and I go on vacation, she gets pregnant. Went to Italy and she got pregnant. Went to Spain and she got pregnant a second time. Went to France and she got pregnant a third time." The doctor says, "Have you ever thought of using any kind of protection to avoid it?" Walter says, "No, I just thought that maybe next time I'd take my wife with me."

Being a doctor is a wonderful way to make a living. The doctor gets a woman to take her clothes off, and then he sends the bill to her husband.

Harvey went to see his doctor. He said, "I'm very worried about my wife. She keeps thinking that she's a bridge." The doctor said, "My goodness, what's come over her?" He said, "Two trucks and a bus."

This dumb girl went to the doctor to have an abortion. The doctor said, "Why do you want an abortion?" She said, "I don't think it's mine."

A doctor examined a woman. He left his office and went over to her husband. The doctor said, "I don't like the looks of your wife." The husband said, "Neither do I, but she's a wonderful cook, and she's great with the kids."

This fellow went to his doctor and said, "My wife is losing all of her sexual desire. Could you give me something for her?" The doctor said, "I have just what she needs. Take these pills, and at dinner slip a couple into her food. You'll have the results you desire." That night at dinner, he slipped a couple of pills in her food. He said, "I'll take a couple myself." They went to bed. At 2:00 in the morning she sat up in bed, and yelled, "I want a man." He woke up and yelled, "Me too, me too!!"

Italian Jokes

An Alitalia Airplane has just taken off from New York bound for Italy. After being in flight for two hours, the pilot made an announcement over the loud speaker: "Ladies and-a gentlemen, dis is-a your pilot, Captain Pasquale talking. I gotta good news, and I gotta bad news. First, di bad-a news. We lost. I don't-a know where the hell-a we are. Now for di good-a news. We makin'-a damn good time."

How do you sink an Italian submarine?
Put it in water

Tony walked into a bank and asked the cashier at the window if he could see the person in charge of loans. The cashier said, "I'm sorry, sir, but the loan arranger is out to lunch." Tony said, "Well, if I can't-a talk-a to the Loan A-ranger, den I talk-a to Tonto!"

What is the thinnest book in the world?
A History of Italian War Heroes

The Mel Simons Joke Book

A man goes into Tony's Barber Shop and sits down in the barber chair. He says, "Listen, Tony, I want you to give me a haircut just like Tom Selleck. I love Tom Selleck, and I want my hair to look just like his." Tony says, "Donju worry. I fix-a you up." Tony starts to cut his hair, and the man falls asleep. He wakes up 30 minutes later, looks in the mirror, and sees that he is completely bald. He says, "Tony, what did you do to me? I'm bald. I asked you for a haircut just like Tom Selleck. Don't you know who Tom Selleck is?" Tony says, "Sure, I used to-a watch-a him all the time-a on-a Kojak!"

What do Italians call the northern part of the United States?
The uppa U.S.

Why did the Italians lose the war?
They used ziti instead of shells

What is the national bird of Italy?
The stool pigeon

Angelo wanted to become a citizen of the United States. He went to court to take his citizenship test. He was very nervous as he stood before the judge. He said, "Mr. Judge-a, your honor, I don't-a think I'm a gonna pass-a di test, because I don't-a talk-a so good." The judge looked down and said, "Donju worry, you ginna pass-a!"

Italian Jokes

An Italian and an Englishman were lost in the middle of the Atlantic Ocean, on a raft. Suddenly, a periscope arose from the water. The Englishman looked up and said, "I say, old chap, is that a U-boat?" The Italian looked and said, "No, it's-a not-a my boat."

An elderly Italian man was on his death bed. His wife, Maria, was by his side. He looks up at his wife, and says, "Maria, I-a remember when-a we first-a get-a married, and-a we have-a no money. You was-a by my side. And-a during during-a the depression, no food-a, no money, and you was-a by my side. Then I have-a big-a auto accident. Broken-a bones, one hundred-a stitches, and you was-a by my side. Now, I'm on-a my death bed, Maria, and you by-a my side. You know some-a thing, Maria, I tink-a you bad-a luck."

What do Italians do with their old, out of style clothing?
They wear them.

A little Italian man walked into a pizza shop and ordered a pizza. The man behind the counter said, "Do you want it cut in six pieces or eight pieces?" He said, "Six. I don't-a think I can-a eat-a eight."

What is an Italian mother's proudest moment?
When her son pulls his first job

The Mel Simons Joke Book

Did you hear about the new Italian university?
It's called "Whatsa Matta U"

What is purple, red, brown, green, yellow, orange, and blue?
An Italian who is all dressed up

A 21 year old man was notified by the draft board that they wanted him in the Army. When he showed the draft notice to his mother, she started to yell, "My little-a boy, my little-a bambino, my bella bambino, dey take-a him in-a dih Army." The son said, "Mom, why are you talking like that? You're not Italian."

What's the first think a student learns from an Italian driving teacher?
How to open a car door without a key

How does the Admiral of the Italian Navy review his fleet?
Through a glass bottom boat

A man went out for lunch. He said to the man behind the counter, "I'd like a meatball sub, provolone cheese, and plenty of garlic." The man behind the counter said, "Hey, buddy, I'll bet you that you're Italian." He said, "C'mon, how did you know? Was it that I ordered a meatball sub?" The counterman said, "No." He said, "Was it the provolone

Italian Jokes

cheese?" The counterman said, "No." He said, "Was it the garlic?" The counterman said, "No." He said, "Then how did you know?" The counterman said, "Because you're in a hardware store."

What do they call the Captain of an Italian submarine?
Chicken of the Sea

Why shouldn't Italian mamas wear yellow?
So people don't yell "TAXI" at them

Bigamist: A fog over Italy

Operetta: A girl who works for the Italian phone company

Why don't the Italians like the Jehovah's Witnesses?
The Italians don't like any witnesses

What's the first thing that they teach the soldiers to do in the Italian Army?
To raise their hands above their heads

Jokes

A terrible actor was on stage appearing in Hamlet. He was awful. He kept forgetting his lines. In the middle of "to be or not to be" he was so bad that the audience started to boo and throw things at him. The actor stopped the show, came to the front of the stage and said, "Listen, folks, I didn't write this crap."

A 99 year old great grandfather married a 98 year old great grandmother. They spent their honeymoon getting out of the car.

Sam and Harry, two old friends, meet in the street. Sam says, "Harry, I just bought a new hearing aid. It cost me three thousand dollars. It's the finest hearing aid that money can buy. It's worth every penny." Harry said, "Really? What kind is it?" Sam said, "It's a quarter to five."

Golf Jokes

Two golfers are on the first tee. One guy takes out a brand new ball, and he hits it in the water. He takes out another brand new ball and hits it over the fence. Another brand new ball, hits it in the water. The other guy said, "Why don't you use an old ball?" He said, "I never had one."

I said to my caddy, "Do you think that it's a sin to play on religious holidays?" He said, "Believe me, any day you play is a sin."

A man goes to a golf course and says, "Look, I can't see good. Get me a caddy with good eyesight. After I hit the ball, I want the caddy to tell me where the ball went." They get him a 90 year old caddy with great eyesight. The man hits the ball. He says to the caddy, "Did you see where the ball went?"
   The caddy says, "Yes." The man says, "Where?" He says, "I don't remember."

A guy is dating a girl. He says, "Look, we're dating a long time. I want you to know one thing. Golf is my great love. I adore the game of golf. I will go anywhere, anytime to play golf. I want you to know that." She says, "You know, I want you to know something. I'm a hooker." He said, "Maybe you're not holding the club right."

Norman and Marty have been pals for years. They both love to play golf.

Norman: "Do you suppose there are golf courses in heaven?"

Marty: "I'm not sure, but the first one of us that gets there should try and contact the other."

Norman dies first. Two weeks later Marty is going out to play golf and he hears a voice. "Hello, Marty. It's Norman speaking to you. I'm in heaven."

Marty: "Is it really you, Norman?"

"Yes," says Norman. "I have good news and bad news for you. First the good news. The golf courses up here are fabulous. Now the bad news. You have a starting time tomorrow at noon."

Jokes

Three old timers are talking about who they would like to be buried with.
First guy: "I would like to be buried with Abraham Lincoln. He was a great president."
Second guy: "I would like to be buried with Albert Einstein. He was a genius."
Third guy: "I would like to be buried with Angelina Jolie."
First guy: "Angelina Jolie? She's not dead."
Third guy: "Neither am I!"

A man says to his barber, "My hair is falling out. What can I use to keep it in?" The barber answers, "I would suggest a shoebox."

A guy goes to a lady psychiatrist. She says, "I am completely booked. I am booked solid for the next two years. What is your problem?" The guy said, "I am extremely oversexed." She said, "I can squeeze you in tonight."

The Mel Simons Joke Book

Bob Hope

Bob Hope Jokes

I grew up with five brothers. That's how I learned how to dance, waiting for the bathroom.

I was able to find my original birth certificate, but it took 3 guys to help me get it. Stone tablets are heavy.

I do benefits for all religions. I'd hate to blow the hereafter on a technicality.

I don't know what people have got against government. They've done nothing.

I play golf in the eighties. Any hotter, I won't play.

A James Cagney love scene is one where he lets the other guy live.

When I was in Vaudeville, I would not have had anything to eat if it wasn't for the stuff the audience threw at me.

The Mel Simons Joke Book

I was called "Rembrandt Hope" in my boxing days, because I spent so much time on the canvas.

I always go to church affairs that I am invited to. I'd better. Once I turned one down, and it snowed in my living room in Palm Springs.

I was the youngest of five boys. After they had me, mom and dad never spoke to each other again.

Long dresses don't bother me. I've got a great memory.

The trees in Siberia are miles apart. That's why the dogs are so fast.

I don't feel old. I don't feel anything until noon. Then it's time for my nap.

I went to a Catholic dinner at the Waldorf once. I knew it was a Catholic church affair. I left my car at the curb, and it was raffled off.

I love flying. I've been to almost as many places as my luggage.

They say that animal behavior can warn you when an earthquake is coming. Like the night before that last earthquake hit, our family dog took the car keys and drove to Arizona.

I love to go to Washington, if only to be near my money.

Bob Hope and Mel Simons

Jokes

A motorcycle cop was stationed by a toll booth. He saw a lady knitting as she waited to pay the toll. As she pulled away, he drove alongside her and yelled, "Pull over." She yelled back, "No, a cardigan."

Two bookies were coming out of church. One said to the other, "The word is hallelujah, not Hialeah!"

A man writes a letter to the Internal Revenue Service. "On my last return I cheated. I've had a guilty conscience ever since. I haven't been able to sleep. Enclosed you'll find my check in the amount of $500. If I still can't sleep, I'll send you the balance."

There was a robbery at the police station. The crooks stole all the toilets. The cops have nothing to go on.

A man checks into a motel. On the nightstand he sees a bible. He picks up the bible, and a card falls out. He looks at the card, and it says, "If you're an alcoholic call this number." He called the number and it was a package store.

I know this veterinarian that loves to breed dogs. He crossed a pit bull with a St. Bernard. He got a dog that attacks you and then goes for help.

Brenda and Bob were out on a date.
Bob: "I want you for my wife."
Brenda: "What would your wife want with me?"

A man is lost in the woods. He comes upon a monastery, a religious building of monks. Many of the friars are working outside. He tells the friars that he is lost, and he is hungry, and they invite him inside. They say that all they have to eat is fish and chips. He loves the fish and chips. He says, "I'd like to meet the man that made the fish." They bring the cook out. The man says, "Are you the fish fryer?" He answered, "No, I'm the chip monk."

Fred and Herbie, two friends meet for lunch. Fred: "I just got a French poodle for my wife." Herbie: "You made a good exchange."

I heard that Christian Brothers just merged with Folgers Coffee. Their new theme song will be called "Onward Christian Folgers."

The Mel Simons Joke Book

Myron Cohen and Mel Simons

Myron Cohen Jokes

An undertaker calls a son-in-law. He says, "About your mother-in-law, do you want us to embalm her, cremate her, or bury her?" He said, "Do all three. Don't take chances."

Four guys are playing gin rummy. One of them loses $800 and drops dead at the table. Out of respect to the deceased, they finish the game standing up. However, the situation now presents a problem. Somebody has to tell his wife. Nobody wants to do it. So they draw lots. One of them is selected, and the other two ask him to be careful breaking the news, be very gentle. So he goes to the man's house, rings the bell. The door opens and he says, "Lady, your husband just lost $800 playing gin." She says, "He should drop dead." He says, "He did!"

An 8 year old girl walks into a bakery and says, "My mommy found a fly in the raisin bread." The baker said, "So bring back the fly and I'll give you a raisin."

A drunk is driving his car the wrong way on a one way street. A copy stops him, and says, "Where the hell do you think you're going? Didn't you see the arrows?" He said, "I didn't even seen the Indians."

Three men are sitting in a restaurant. They each ordered a glass of milk. One of them said to the waiter, "Make sure my glass is clean." Three minutes later the waiter came back and says, "Which one ordered the clean glass?"

Two ladies meet in a beauty parlor.
First lady: "Where did you go last season?"
Second lady: "We went to Majorca."
First lady: "Where's that?"
Second lady: "I don't know. We flew."

A five year old boy says to his friend, "My father can beat up your father." The friend says, "Big deal. So can my mother."

Two business partners are in conversation. One says, "What do you think about the Taft Hartley Bill?" The other one says, "The hell with it, pay it."

This little lady is on her death bed. The end is near. The husband is by her bed side. She says, "Morris, tomorrow for the funeral, do me a favor. Let my mother ride with you in the first funeral car." He said, "No way." She said, "Please, Morris, it's my last request." He said, "Let her drop dead and go with you in your car."

Husband and wife having breakfast.

Wife: "You know that family that moved into the house across the street? They are a lovely couple. Every morning when he's leaving for work, they stand in the doorway and they hug and they kiss. On his way to the car, he keeps on waiving and throwing kisses. Why don't you do this?"

He says, "I don't know the woman!"

Two ladies having lunch.

First lady: "Where did you go for vacation last year?"

Second lady: "We took a cruise around the world. Next year we're going someplace else."

A man calls an undertaker and says, "You better come to my house and make arrangements for the funeral. My wife passed away." The undertaker said, "What are you talking about? I buried your wife three years ago." He said, "Yes, but I got married again." The undertaker said, "Oh, congratulations!"

Books

Seven books that will never be published:

Ten Thousand Years of German Humor

Irish Gourmet Cooking

Blacks I Have Met While Yachting

Italian War Heroes

Famous Jews In The World Of Hockey

How To Remove Your Appendix In Your Spare Time

Brain Surgery Self Taught

Signs

Sign in a dentist's office:
"Be true to your teeth or they will be false to you."

Sign at a Las Vegas dice table:
"Shake well before losing."

Sign in a maternity store:
"20% discount for seniors"

Sign in a doctor's office:
"The doctor is very busy. Please have your symptoms ready."

Sign on a cesspool truck:
"A flush is better than a full house."

The Mel Simons Joke Book

Rodney Dangerfield

Rodney Dangerield Jokes

I come from a very confused family. In the Civil War, my great grandfather fought for the west.

I was so ugly as a kid, on Halloween I had to play trick or treat over the phone.

When I was a kid, I got no respect. One time I was kidnapped, and the kidnappers sent my parents a note. They said, "We want $5000 or you'll see your kid again."

We once went to the beach. My father gave the lifeguard $10 to keep his eye off me.

I live in a tough neighborhood. We just put up a sign. It says, "Drive fast. The life you save may be your own."

You know that dinner is ready in my house when the smoke alarm goes off.

I have no self-confidence. If a girl tells me yes, I tell her to think it over.

I tell you, with my doctor, I don't get no respect. I told him, "I've swallowed a bottle of sleeping pills." He told me to have a few drinks and get some rest."

When I was a kid I played hide-and-seek, and no one came to look for me.

I get no respect. I recently bought a cemetery plot. The guy said, "There goes the neighborhood."

My mother never breast fed me. She told me that she only liked me as a friend.

I once appeared in a place that was so far out in the woods, my act was reviewed in Field and Stream.

I get no respect. I once stayed at a hotel and left a wake-up call for the next morning. They missed by a day and a half.

My wife is the worst cook in the world. In my house you pray after you eat.

A girl phoned me last week and said, "Come on over, there's nobody home." So I went over. There was nobody home.

My wife met me at the door wearing a see-through negligee. Unfortunately, she was just coming home.

With my dog I get no respect. He keeps barking at the front door. He doesn't want to go out. He wants me to leave.

I told my wife the truth. I told her I was seeing a psychiatrist. Then she told me the truth. She was seeing a psychiatrist, two plumbers, and a butcher.

Simons Sez

Live each day like it was your last and then one day you'll be right.

Never go to a bank and get in line behind someone wearing a ski mask.

Beauty is only skin deep, but ugly is right to the bone.

My Aunt Bessie was a very strange woman. She buried three husbands, and two of them were just napping.

He who turns the other cheek will be hit with the other fist.

Be true to your teeth, and they won't be false to you.

Those who live by the sword get shot by those who don't.

Always try to keep a smile on your face because it looks silly on other parts of your body.

Let he who hath a bad kidney cast the first stone.

Marriage is like a warm bath. After you get used to it, it's not so hot.

A closed mouth gathers no foot.

As you slide down the banister of life, may all the splinters be pointing the right way.

When arguing with a stupid person, make sure he's not doing the same thing.

When I read about the evils of drinking, I gave up reading.

When you go to court, you're putting yourself in the hands of twelve people who weren't smart enough to get out of jury duty.

Ninety percent of accidents occur within a mile of home. So I moved.

Never go to bed mad. Stay up and fight.

A verbal contract isn't worth the paper it's written on.

Simons Asks

If a turtle loses its shell, is it homeless or naked?

How come Kamikaze pilots always wear helmets?

How can you tell when you're out of invisible ink?

What do you send to a sick florist?

Why do they lock gas station bathrooms? Are they concerned that someone will clean them?

Why do they sterilize needles for lethal injections?

Why do hot dogs come in packages of 10 and buns in packages of 8?

How come Superman stops a bullet with his chest, but ducks when something is thrown at him?

Simons Asks

In the newspaper's obituary column, how come everybody dies in alphabetical order?

Why don't you ever see the headline "Psychic wins lottery?"

Why is lemon juice made with artificial flavor and dishwashing liquid made with real lemons?

How come people will order a triple cheeseburger, large fries, and a diet coke?

Why is a boxing ring square?

If a mute swears, does his mother wash his hands with soap?

Why is it necessary to nail down the lid of a coffin?

If nothing sticks to Teflon, how does it stay on the pan?

The Mel Simons Joke Book

Sam Levenson

Sam Levenson Jokes

The reason grandparents and grandchildren get along so well is that they have a common enemy.

I'm going to stop putting things off, starting tomorrow.

When I was growing up, our menu at mealtime offered two choices: take it or leave it.

It was on my fifth birthday that Papa put his hand on my shoulder and said, "Remember, my son, if you ever need a helping hand, you'll find one at the end of your arm."

Lead us not into temptation, just tell us where it is, we'll find it.

If you die in an elevator, be sure to push the up button.

If your wife wants to learn to drive, don't stand in her way.

The Mel Simons Joke Book

When I was a boy, I used to do what my father wanted. Now I have to do what my boy wants. My problem is, when am I going to do what I want?

Love at first sight is easy to understand. It's when two people have been looking at each other for a lifetime that it becomes a miracle.

I have always laughed at my own jokes, not because I think they are funny, but because Papa had told me, "Never depend on strangers."

Somewhere on this earth, every ten seconds, there is a woman giving birth to a child. She must be found and stopped.

You must learn from the mistakes of others. You can't possibly live long enough to make them all yourself.

It's so simple to be wise. Just think of something stupid to say, and then don't say it.

At the end of the day, Mama could count on Papa to come home with those three little words on his lips that made it all worthwhile: "What's for supper?"

Sam Levenson Jokes

You must pay for your sins. If you have already paid, please ignore this notice.

I discovered that if I move the bathroom scale to a room where the floor slants a little, I can lose weight without struggling.

Jokes

A fellow walks into a bar and says, "Who owns that big German Shepherd tied up outside?" A big lumberjack says, "I do." The man said, "Well, my dog just killed it." The lumberjack said, "Your dog just killed my German Shepherd? Are you crazy? My Shepherd is an attack dog." The man said, "I don't care. My dog killed it." The lumberjack said, "What kind of a dog do you have?" The man said, "A Chihuahua." The lumberjack said, "Your Chihuahua killed my German Shepherd? How did he do that?" The man said, "He got stuck in his throat."

A couple have been married for twenty five years. One day the husband says, "Mildred, why don't we go on a vacation?" As he says this, he looks into the living room and sees a little old lady knitting. He says, "If you don't mind, let's go without your mother this time." She says, "My mother? I thought she was your mother!"

Lawyer Jokes

How do you save a drowning lawyer?
Take your foot off his head.

Why are there so many toxic dump sites in New Jersey, and so many lawyers in Washington?
New Jersey had first choice.

A lawyer was walking down the street and saw an auto accident. He rushed over, started handing out business cards, and said, "I saw the whole thing. I'll take either side."

A guy walks into a bar and yells, "All lawyers are morons. Show me a lawyer, and I'll show you a moron." Another guy in the back yells out, "Hey, I resent that remark." "Why? Are you a lawyer?" "No, I'm a moron."

What do you get when you cross the Godfather with a lawyer?
An offer you can't understand

What do you call 500 lawyers lying on the bottom of the sea?
A good start

The Mel Simons Joke Book

What's the difference between a lawyer and a herd of buffalo?
A lawyer charges more

What do you say to a lawyer with an IQ of 50?
Good morning, your honor.

How can you tell when a lawyer is lying?
His lips are moving.

Why do they bury lawyers 100 feet into the ground?
Because, down deep, they're good people.

What's the difference between a vulture and a lawyer?
Wing tips

What does a lawyer use for birth control?
His personality

A man was on trial from Alaska. The lawyer turned to him and asked, "Where were you on the night of October to April?"

An electrician was doing some wiring for a lawyer. When he finished, he handed the lawyer a bill for $500. The lawyer

Lawyer Jokes

said, "That's a lot of money for an hour's work. I'm a lawyer, and I don't get that much." "Funny," said the electrician. "When I was a lawyer, I didn't either."

Two lawyers were going at each other as the trial was about to begin. One lawyer said to the other, "You're a bum. You're a total fraud." The other lawyer said, "You're a moron. You're a penny stealing ambulance chaser." The judge interrupted, saying, "Now that you've identified one another, shall we go on with the case?"

What's black and brown and looks good on a lawyer?
A Doberman

The Mel Simons Joke Book

Buddy Hackett

Buddy Hackett Jokes

Last week I was driving my car and I hit a motorcycle cop. He walked over to me with a big grin on his face. The grin was from ear to ear. He had the handlebars stuck in his mouth.

I went to see the doctor. I said, "Doc, it's my foot. I can't walk." He said, "You'll be walking before the day is through." He took my car!

I married a very young wife. She was seventeen when we got married. I didn't know whether to take her on a honeymoon or send her to camp.

All my wife wants from my life is to take out the garbage. When I'm away on a trip, she mails me the garbage.

The Mel Simons Joke Book

Steve Allen

Steve Allen Jokes

A guy walks into a saloon with a duck under his arm. The bartender says, "What are you doing with that pig?" The guy says, "What are you talking about? This is not a pig. This is a duck." The bartender says, "I was talking to the duck."

When I was a kid I was very absent minded. I played hooky from school on weekends.

An airplane was in flight over the Pacific. There were mechanical problems and they had to lighten their load. The pilot asked for three volunteers to bail out. A Frenchman stood up and shouted, "Vive La France" and he jumped out. An Englishman stood up and shouted, "Long live the Queen" and he jumped out. A Texan stood up and shouted, "Remember the Alamo" and he pushed a Mexican out.

Jokes

A five year old boy walked over to his grandfather and said, "Grandpa, will you make the noise of a frog?" The grandfather said, "Where did you hear that I can make the noise of a frog?" The little boy said, "I just heard Mommy tell Daddy that when you croak, we will all go to Disneyland."

So this patient says to his proctologist, "What made you become a proctologist?" The proctologist answered, "I can't remember faces."

A turtle is crossing the street. Suddenly he is mugged by two snails. The cops show up and they ask the turtle, "What happened?" The turtle said, "I'm not sure. It happened so fast."

Las Vegas is the most religious city in the world. Any hour, day or night, you can walk into a casino and hear someone say, "Oh, my God!"

Jewish Jokes

A German, a Frenchman, and a Jew are lost in the desert. The German says, "I'm tired and I'm thirsty. I must have beer." The Frenchman said, "I'm tired and I'm thirsty. I must have wine." The Jew said, "I'm tired and I'm thirsty. I must have diabetes."

Why do Jewish men die before their wives?
They want to

Anytime a non-Jewish person goes into a delicatessen and orders a corned beef sandwich on white bread with mayonnaise, somewhere in the world a Jew dies.

The doctor called one of his patients on the telephone. He said, "Mrs. Goldberg, your check, it came back." She said, "So did my arthritis!"

Six Jewish women were having lunch in a restaurant. Halfway through the meal, the waitress walked over and asked, "Is anything all right?"

Did you hear about the Jewish Robin Hood?
He steals from the rich and he keeps it.

I recently rented a car in Miami Beach. It came with a Jewish GPS. It kept asking me, "Did you eat today?"

Why do Jewish divorces cost so much?
They're worth it

A Jewish boy comes home from school and tells his mother he has a part in the school play. She asks, "What part do you have?" The boy says, "I play the part of a Jewish husband." She says, "Go back and tell the teacher that you want a speaking part."

If a Jewish married man is walking in the woods and he is talking and nobody hears him, is he still wrong?

Two bees are flying next to each other. One of the bees is wearing a yarmulke. The other bee said, "You're a bee. Why are you wearing a yarmulke on your head?" The bee said, "I don't want people to think I'm a wasp."

Why isn't there a Jewish woman on the parole board?
Because she would never let a man finish his sentence

Jewish Jokes

Near my house there is a new Jewish-Chinese restaurant. It's called SO-SUE ME.

Did you hear about the Jewish mother that was a travel agent for guilt trips?

A car hit an elderly Jewish man. He was lying in the street. The paramedic said to him, "Are you comfortable?" The man said, "I make a good living."

Jewish porno film: *Debbie Does Dishes*

Why can't you keep Jews in jail?
Because they eat Lox

Jewish-Mexican restaurant: The Casa Hadassah

Harvey Cohen called his mother in Miami Beach. He said, "Mom, how are you feeling?" She said, "I'm not feeling good. I'm very weak." He said, "Why are you weak?" She said, "Because I haven't eaten for fifty five days. He said, "Why have you not eaten for fifty five days?" She said, "Because I didn't want my mouth to be filled with food in case you called."

The Mel Simons Joke Book

Two elderly Jewish men are sitting on a bench in Central Park. The first man says, "I am so happy. My son just graduated from law school." The second man asked, "NYU?" The first man answered, "And why not?"

Rabbi Margolis became ill quite suddenly and was rushed to Beth Israel Hospital. He was operated on for gall bladder. The next day, several members of his temple came to visit. They said, "Rabbi, we are representing the board of trustees at the temple. They wish you a complete recovery by a vote of 7 to 3.

A little Jewish woman bought two live chickens. One got sick, so she killed the healthy one to make chicken soup for the sick one

A little old Jewish man is sitting by the pool in Florida. A little old lady comes over to him and says, "Excuse me, mister. You're sitting by the pool. Why are you looking so pale?" He says, "I've been away." She says, "Where have you been?" He says, "I've been in jail." She says, "What did you do?" He says, "I cut my wife up into little pieces and buried her in the backyard." She looks at him for a few seconds and says, "So that means you're single?"

What does a Jewish American Princess make for dinner? Reservations

Jewish Jokes

A tourist was visiting Hawaii. He walked over to an elderly Jewish man and asked, "Excuse me, sir. Is this state pronounced Hawaii or Havaii?" The old man said, "Havaii." The tourist said, "Thank you." The old man said, "You're velcome."

Two old friends are talking. One says to the other, "I've got a great joke for you that I just heard. Two Jews meet and one says…" The other guy says, "Wait a minute. Why is it that whenever you begin a joke it's always two Jews? Why can't it be two Italians, or two Frenchmen, or better yet, two Chinamen?" He says "All right, don't get excited. Two Chinamen meet, and one says to the other, 'Noo, Max, are you coming home for Passover this year?'"

My old friend, Van Harris, the great comedian, tells this wonderful story. An American Indian girl marries a Jewish boy and both families are very upset. The Indian girl's parents said, "What did she marry a Jew for?" The Jewish boy's parents said, "Why did he marry an Indian?" Finally both families realized that love conquers all, and the marriage was accepted. A year later, they had a baby, and the arguing started again. The Indian girl's parents said, "That's an Indian baby. The baby should have an Indian name." The Jewish boy's parents said, "The baby's a Jew. The baby should have a Jewish name." Fortunately, level heads prevailed. They compromised and named the baby Whitefish.

The Mel Simons Joke Book

What do you call a Japanese girl who marries a Jewish man? An Orienta

There is a very swank synagogue in Beverly Hills, California. On Yom Kippur there is a sign in front of the synagogue: "Closed for the Jewish Holidays!"

A priest, and minister, and a rabbi are talking about how they divided up the money that is contributed to them. The priest says, "What we do is make a great big circle. Then we throw the money up in the air. Whatever lands inside the circle is for the Lord. Whatever lands outside the circle is for us." The minister says, "What we do is make a long straight line. Then we throw the money up in the air. Whatever falls to the right of the line is for the Lord. Whatever falls to the left of the line is for us." The rabbi says, "What we do is throw the money up in the air. Whatever the Lord wants, He takes."

Jokes

Two little ladies meet in the street. One says to the other, "What did you do to your hair? It looks like a wig." The other one says, "It is a wig." The first one says, "You know, you could never tell!"

A man applies for a job in the Post Office. They give him a questionnaire to fill out. The first question was, "How far is it from the earth to the moon?" He said, "If that's the route, I don't want the job."

Two kangaroos meet in the forest. One says to the other, "Gee, I hope it doesn't rain today. I just hate it when the kids play inside."

A man calls his local hospital. He says, "I need help right away. Please help me. My wife is going into labor." The nurse said, "Sir, please calm down. Is this her first child?" He said, "No, this is her husband."

Husband and wife in bed at night. Husband: "The fun and sex has gone out of our marriage." Wife: "Let's discuss it during the next commercial."

The Mel Simons Joke Book

Irving went to an exorcist. He said, "You've got to help me. I'm going crazy." The exorcist said, "What seems to be the problem?" Irving said, "There was a curse put on me 35 years ago. I've suffered all these years. Please remove this curse." The exorcist said, "What were the words that were used in this curse?" Irving said, "I now pronounce you man and wife."

My old pal, former wrestling champion Walter "Killer" Kowalski, loves to tell this one:

> Did you hear about the guy that was half Polish and half Jewish?
> He's a janitor, but he owns the building.

My Brother-In-Law

I have a brother-in-law named Bernie. He is a wonderful person, but many unusual things have happened throughout his life:

Bernie's parents never liked him. When he was born, his mother asked, "Will he live?" The doctor said, "Only if you take your foot off his throat."

Shortly after he was born he became the poster boy for birth control.

When he was eight months old he had memorized the entire Encyclopedia Britannica, but he couldn't talk, so nobody knew.

When Bernie was a kid he loved to play hide and seek. One time he hid in the closet and his family moved.

Once, when he was 9 years old, this father took him aside and left him there.

The Mel Simons Joke Book

When Bernie was growing up, he used to play spin the bottle. If the girls didn't want to kiss him, they had to pay him a quarter. By the time he was 11 years old he owned his own home.

He went to a tough high school. He had friends with names like Rocky, Killer and Mad Dog. And those were the cheerleaders.

Bernie was once mugged in a library. He had to whisper for help.

He was mugged a second time by a bus driver. Luckily the bus driver didn't get Bernie's money because Bernie didn't have the exact change.

Twice Bernie was run over by a Welcome Wagon. Once when his mother was driving, and once when his father was driving.

As an adult, he built a home for runaway girls and he ran away with two of them.

He once went for jury duty and was found guilty.

Recently Bernie willed his body to science. Science has contested the will.

Fat Jokes

You know you are overweight when you sit in your bathtub and the water in the toilet rises.

My friend, Paul, has taken up horseback riding to lose weight, and it's working. So far the horse has lost forty pounds.

He recently went on a three week diet. He lost twenty one days.

He is so fat that when he gets in an elevator, it has to go down.

Paul's high school yearbook photo is on page 60, 61, and half of 62.

When he goes through a revolving door, he has to make two trips.

The Mel Simons Joke Book

Jokes

My favorite delicatessen is Evan's Deli in Marblehead, Massachusetts. A Martian was in his flying saucer and he landed in front of Evan's Deli. As the flying saucer landed, he got a flat tire. Unfortunately, he had no spare. He began looking in store windows to see if he could get a spare tire. He looked in the window of Evan's Deli and saw a bunch of bagels. He said, "Oh boy, there's one of those spare tires." So he went in and said to Evan, "I want to buy one of those tires." Evan said, "What, are you crazy? That's not a tire, that's a bagel." The Martian said, "What's a bagel?" Evan said, "Here, taste one." The Martian bit into it and said, "You know, this would be great with cream cheese and lox!"

Jack and Fred meet for dinner. Jack says, "You look terrible. What's the problem?" Fred says, "I lost three wives in the past seven months." Jack says, "What happened?" Fred says, "My first wife died from eating poison mushrooms." Jack says, "What happened to your second wife?" Fred says, "She died from eating poison mushrooms." Jack says, "What happened to your third wife?" Fred says, "She wouldn't eat the poison mushrooms."

Knock-Knock Jokes

Knock, knock.
  Who's there?
Diploma
  Diploma who?
Diploma is here to fix the sink

Knock, knock.
  Who's there?
Butcher
  Butcher who?
Butcher arms around me, honey

Knock, knock.
  Who's there?
Sam and Janet
  Sam and Janet who?
Sam and Janet evening

Knock, knock.
  Who's there?
Owen
  Owen who?
Owen the saints go marching in

The Mel Simons Joke Book

Joey Bishop

Joey Bishop Jokes

My family was so poor, we couldn't give my sister a sweet sixteen party until she was twenty eight.

Today you can go to a gas station and find the cash register open and the toilet locked.

In kindergarten I flunked sand pile.

Customer: "I'd like some rat poison."
Clerk: "Will you take it with you?"
Customer: "No, I'll send the rats over to get it."

My wife will buy anything marked down. Yesterday she tried to buy an escalator.

I have a wonderful doctor. Once, when I couldn't afford an operation, he touched up the x-rays.

The Mel Simons Joke Book

George Burns

George Burns Jokes

Every morning when I get up, I read the obituary page. If my name is not there, I shave.

Jack Benny is my closest friend. I'd give him the shirt off my back. He'd wash it, iron it, and charge me $5.

I'm at the age now where just putting my cigar in its holder is a thrill.

You know you're getting old when you bend over to tie your shoelaces and wonder what else you could do while you're down there.

It takes only one drink to get me drunk. The trouble is, I can't remember if it's the thirteenth or the fourteenth.

Happiness is having a large, loving, caring, close knit family in another city.

The Mel Simons Joke Book

The secret of a good sermon is to have a good beginning and a good ending. Then have the two as close together as possible.

I smoke cigars because at my age, if I don't have something to hang onto, I might fall down.

I'm so old that the other night I went to see a porno picture with Jack Benny. We both fell asleep.

First you forget names, then you forget faces. Next you forget to pull your zipper up, and finally you forget to pull it down.

You know you're old when everybody goes to your birthday party and stands around the cake just to get warm.

Jokes

Two women were talking. One said to the other, "Did you hear what happened to Julie? She got mixed up with what's-his-name, and then she got involved with you-know-who, and you should see what happened to her with what-do-you-call-it. I told you this story before, didn't I?" "Yes, but this is the first time I heard all the details."

Epitaph on the tombstone of a hypochondriac: "I told you I was sick."

A man walks into a barber shop and says to the barber, "How many ahead of me?" The barber says, "Six." And the man walks out. All week long the man does this. At the end of the week, the barber says to the shoe shine boy, "Follow that guy. See where he goes." The shoe shine boy comes back twenty minutes later and says, "He goes to your house."

The Mel Simons Joke Book

Old Age Jokes

You know you're getting old when...

Your friends compliment you on your alligator shoes, and you're walking around barefoot.

You get out of breath playing checkers.

You still chase women, but forget why.

You know your way around, but you don't feel like going.

A good looking gal walks by, and your pacemaker opens the garage door.

You missed your afternoon nap. You slept right through it.

You can remember when the Dead Sea was only sick.

Your Cream of Wheat is too spicy.

A pregnant woman offers you her seat on the bus.

Your wife says, "Let's go upstairs and make love," and you say, "Honey, I can't do both."

Old Age Jokes

Your legs buckle, and your belt doesn't.

You found out that your blood type has been discontinued.

You realize that you were a busboy at the Last Supper.

Bingo has become a spectator sport.

Your back goes out more than you do.

Your birthday cake collapses from the weight of the candles.

A woman buys a sheer nightie and doesn't know anyone who can see through it.

You pay for sex and get a refund.

It takes a couple of times to go over a speed bump.

You get into your car and the steering wheel is higher than you are.

You sit in a rocking chair and you can't get it started.

You feel like the morning after and you haven't been anywhere.

The Mel Simons Joke Book

Your wife gives up sex for lent and you don't realize it until the 4th of July.

You order a martini with a prune instead of an olive.

Your secrets are safe because your friends don't remember them either.

A fortune teller offers to read your face.

Happy Hour is a nap.

You look forward to a dull evening.

You remember that you sat behind Jesus in the second grade.

Jokes

Football game: The Chicago Bears played the New York Jets. Late in the 4th quarter, a passing car backfired. The Jets, thinking the game was over, left the field. Four plays later, the Bears scored.

A man went into a hospital for a heart transplant. The doctors took the heart of a turtle and put it into the man. It worked perfectly. A week after the operation, the man left the hospital. Five weeks later he got to his car.

A ventriloquist is entertaining with the dummy on his lap. He starts to tell a dumb blonde joke. A blonde gal jumps up and yells, "Why are you telling dumb blonde jokes? We happen to be very smart people." The ventriloquist starts to apologize. She yells, "You keep out of this. I was talking to that little fellow on your lap."

CPSIA information can be obtained at www.ICGtesting.com
Printed in the USA
BVOW020742140613

323330BV00004B/6/P